Even More Stories from the Old Testament for Children

Matty Robins

THIS BOOK BELONGS TO_____

"Suffer the little children to come unto me, and forbid them not: for of such is the kingdom of God"

For information about permission to reproduce selections from this book, write to Permissions. The Light and the Way Books.

6845 Elm Street, McLean Va. 22101

Visit our Web site: WWW. Litchfield Literary Books.Com

PREFACE

"The Children's Bible" provides, in simple English, a translation of selections from both the Old and the New Testament. These selections have been made as a result of more than twenty-five years of observation and study. The text is that of the Bible itself, but in the language of the child, so that it may easily be read to the younger children and by those who are older. It is not in words of one syllable, for while the child is reading the Bible he should gradually learn the meaning of new words and idioms.

The Bible contains the foundations on which the religious life of the child must be built. The immortal stories and songs of the Old and New Testaments are his richest inheritance from the past. To give him this heritage in language and form that he can understand and enjoy is the duty and privilege of his parents and teachers.

It is hoped that "The Children's Bible" will meet the need and the demand, which parents and educators alike have long felt and often expressed, for a simple translation of selections from the Bible most suited to the needs and the interests of the child. It is also believed that after the child has learned to appreciate and love these stories and songs, he will be eager and able to read the Bible as a whole with genuine interest and understanding.

THE DEVOTION OF RUTH

During the days of the judges, there was once a famine in the land; and a certain man from Bethlehem in Judah took his wife and two sons to live in the territory of Moab. His name was Elimelech and his wife's Naomi, and his two sons were Mahlon and Chilion. After they had been living in Moab for some time, Elimelech died, and Naomi was left with her two sons. They married Moabite women, named Orpah and Ruth. After they had lived there about ten years, Mahlon and Chilion both died, and Naomi was left without husband or children.

So she set out with her daughters-in-law to return from the land of Moab, for she had heard that Jehovah had remembered his people and given them food. As they were setting out on the journey to Judah, Naomi said to her daughters-in-law, "Go, return each of you to the home of your mother. May Jehovah be kind to you, as you have been kind to the dead and to me. Jehovah grant that each of you may find peace and happiness in the house of a new husband."

Then she kissed them; but they began to weep aloud and said to her, "No, we will return with you to your people." But Naomi said, "Go back, my daughters; why should you go with me? Can I still have sons who might become your husbands? Go back, my daughters, go your own way, for I am too old to have a husband. Even if I should say, 'I have hope,' even if I should have a husband to-night and should have sons, would you wait for them until they were grown up? Would you remain single for them? No, my daughters! I am sorry for you, for Jehovah has afflicted me." Then they again wept aloud, and Orpah kissed her mother-in-law good-by, but Ruth stayed with her.

Naomi said, "See, your sister-in-law is going back to her own people and to her own gods; go along with her!" But Ruth answered, "Do not urge me to leave you or to go back, for wherever you go I will go, and wherever you stay I will stay; your people shall be my people, and your God my God; I will die where you die and be buried there. May Jehovah bring a curse upon me, if anything but death separate you and me." When Naomi saw that Ruth had made up her mind to go with her, she ceased urging her to return.

So they travelled on until they came to Bethlehem. When they arrived there, the whole town was interested, and the women said, "Is this Naomi?" But she said to them, "Do not call me Naomi which means Sweetness: call me Mara which means Bitterness, for the Almighty has given me a bitter lot. I had plenty when I left, but Jehovah has brought me back empty-handed. Why should you call me Naomi, now that Jehovah has turned against me, and the Almighty has afflicted me?" So Naomi and Ruth returned from Moab; and they came to Bethlehem at the beginning of the barley harvest.

Now Naomi was related through her husband to Boaz, a very wealthy man of the family of Elimelech. Ruth, the Moabitess, said to Naomi, "Let me now go into the fields and pick up the scattered heads of grain after him whose favor I should win." Naomi said to her, "Go, my daughter."

So she went to pick up grain in the field after the reapers; and it was
her good fortune to pick up grain in that part of the field which
belonged to Boaz, who was of the family of Elimelech. When Boaz come
from Bethlehem and said to the reapers, "Jehovah be with you," they
answered him, "May Jehovah bless you." Then Boaz said to his servant who
had charge of the reapers, "Whose maiden is this?" The servant replied,
"It is the Moabite maiden who came back with Naomi from the land of
Moab; and she said, 'Let me pick up the scattered grain and gather
sheaves after the reapers.' So she came and has worked all the time
until now, and she has not rested a moment in the field."

Then Boaz said to Ruth, "Listen, my daughter. Do not go to pick up grain
in another field nor leave this place, but stay here with my maidens. I
have told the young men not to trouble you. When you are thirsty, go to
the jars and drink of that which the young men have drawn."

Then she bowed low and said to him, "Why are you so kind to me, to take
interest in me who am from another land?" Boaz replied, "I have heard
what you have done for your mother-in-law since the death of your
husband, and how you left your father and mother and your native land to
come to a people that you did not know before. May Jehovah repay you for
what you have done, and may you be fully rewarded by the God of Israel,
under whose wings you have come to take refuge." Then she said, "I trust
I may please you, my lord, for you have comforted me and spoken kindly
to your servant, although I am not really equal to one of your own
servants."

At noonday Boaz said to her, "Come here and eat some of the food and dip your piece of bread in the wine." So she sat beside the reapers; and he passed her the roasted grain, and she ate until she had had enough and had some left. When she rose to gather grain, Boaz gave this order to his young men: "Let her gather grain even among the sheaves and do not disturb her. Also pull out some for her from the bundles and leave it for her to gather and do not find fault with her."

So she gathered grain in the field until evening, then beat out that which she had gathered; and it was about a bushel of barley. Then she took it up and went into the city and showed her mother-in-law what she had gathered. She also brought out and gave her that which she had left from her meal after she had had enough.

Her mother-in-law said to her, "Where did you gather grain to-day and where did you work? A blessing on him who took interest in you!" Then she told her mother-in-law where she had worked, and said, "The name of the man with whom I worked to-day is Boaz." Naomi said to her daughter-in-law, "May the blessing of Jehovah rest upon him who has not ceased to show his love to the living and to the dead." Naomi also said to her, "The man is a near relative of ours." Ruth the Moabitess added, "He said to me, 'You must keep near my young men until they have completed all my harvest.'" Naomi said to Ruth, "It is best, my daughter, that you should go out with his maidens and that no one should find you in another field." So she gathered grain with the maidens of Boaz until the end of the barley and wheat harvest; but she lived with her mother-in-law.

Then Naomi said to her, "My daughter, shall I not try to find a home for you where you will be happy and contented? Is not Boaz, with whose maidens you have been, a relative of ours? This very night he is going to winnow barley on the threshing-floor. So bathe and anoint yourself and put on your best clothes and go down to the threshing-floor; but do not make yourself known to the man until he is through eating and drinking. Then when he lies down, you mark the place where he lies. Go in, uncover his feet, lie down, and then he will tell you what to do." Ruth said to her, "I will do as you say."

So she went down to the threshing-floor and did just as her mother-in-law told her. When Boaz was through eating and drinking and was in a happy mood, he went to lie down at the end of the heap of grain. Then Ruth came softly and uncovered his feet and lay down. At midnight the man was startled and turned over, and there was a woman lying at his feet. He said, "Who are you?" She answered, "I am Ruth your servant; spread therefore your skirt over your servant, for you are a near relative." He said, "May you be blest by Jehovah, my daughter; for you have shown me greater favor now than at first, for you have not followed young men, whether poor or rich. My daughter, have no fear; I will do for you all that you ask; for all my townsmen know that you are a good woman. Now it is true that I am a near relative; yet there is one nearer than I. Stay here to-night, and then in the morning, if he will marry you, well, let him do it. But if he, being your nearest relative, will not marry you, then as surely as Jehovah lives, I will do so. Lie down until morning."

So she lay at his feet until morning, but rose before any one could tell who she was, for Boaz said, "Let it not be known that a woman came to the threshing-floor." He also said, "Bring the cloak which you have on and hold it." So she held it while he poured into it six measures of barley and laid it on her shoulders. Then he went into the city.

When Ruth came to her mother-in-law, Naomi said, "Is it you, my daughter?" Then Ruth told Naomi all that the man had done for her. She said, "He gave me these six measures of barley; for he said, 'Do not go to your mother-in-law empty-handed.'" Naomi said, "Wait quietly, my daughter, until you know how this will turn out, for the man will not rest unless he settles it all to-day."

Then Boaz went up to the gate and sat down. Just then the near relative of whom Boaz had spoken came along. To him Boaz said, "Ho!" calling him by name, "come here and sit down." So he stopped and sat down. Boaz also took ten of the town elders and said, "Sit down here." So they sat down.

Then he said to the near relative, "Naomi, who has come back from the country of Moab, is offering for sale the piece of land which belonged to our relative Elimelech, and I thought that I would lay the matter before you, and ask you to buy it in the presence of these men who sit here and of the elders of my people. If you will buy it and so keep it in the family, do so; but if not, then tell me, that I may know; for no one but you has the right to buy it, and I am next to you." He said, "I will buy it."

Then Boaz said, "On the day you buy the field from Naomi, you must also marry Ruth the Moabitess, the widow of Mahlon, that a son may be born to bear his name and to receive this field." The near relative said, "I cannot buy it for myself, for fear I should lose what already belongs to me. You take my right of buying it as a relative, for I cannot do so."

Now in those days this was the custom in Israel: to make an agreement between two men the one drew off his shoe and gave it to the other. So when the near relative said to Boaz, "Buy it for yourself," Boaz drew off the man's shoe.

Then Boaz said to the elders and to all the people, "You are witnesses at this time that I have bought all that was Elimelech's and all that was Chilion's and Mahlon's from Naomi. Moreover, I have secured Ruth, the Moabitess, the widow of Mahlon, to be my wife so that she may have a son who will receive this land and carry on Mahlon's name. You are witnesses this day."

Then all the people who were at the gate and the elders said, "We are witnesses. May Jehovah make the woman who is coming into your house like Rachel and Leah, and make you also famous in Bethlehem."

So Boaz married Ruth, and she became his wife; and Jehovah gave to her a son. Then the women said to Naomi, "Blessed be Jehovah who has not left you at this time without a near relative, and may his name be famous in

Israel. This child will bring back your strength and take care of you in your old age; for your daughter-in-law who loves you, who is worth more to you than seven sons, has a son!"

So Naomi took the child in her arms and she became its nurse. Her neighbors also said, "Naomi has a son!" and they named him Obed; he became the father of Jesse, who was the father of David.

SAMUEL THE BOY PROPHET

Elkanah, a Zuphite of the hill country of Ephraim, lived at Ramah with his two wives, Hannah and Peninnah. Peninnah had children, but Hannah had none.

This man used to go up from his village each year to worship and offer a sacrifice to Jehovah of hosts at Shiloh. Whenever the day came for Elkanah to offer a sacrifice he gave portions to his wife Peninnah and to all his sons and daughters; but although he loved Hannah, he gave her only one portion, for Jehovah had given her no children. Peninnah made her angry by mocking her, for Jehovah had given her no children. Elkanah did this year after year; but whenever Hannah went up to the temple of Jehovah, Peninnah made her so angry that she wept and would not eat. So Elkanah her husband said to her, "Hannah, why do you weep and why do you not eat? Why are you so troubled? Am I not more to you than ten sons?"

After they had eaten in Shiloh, Hannah arose and stood before the temple of Jehovah, while Eli the priest was sitting on his seat beside the door posts of the temple. With a sad heart she prayed earnestly to Jehovah and wept bitterly. She also made this sacred promise:

"O Jehovah of hosts!
If thou wilt look at my affliction,
And remember, not forgetting thy servant,
But wilt give thy servant a son,

Then I will give him to thee,

Throughout all the days of his life;

And no razor shall touch his head."

While she continued praying before Jehovah, Eli watched her mouth. She
spoke to herself; her lips moved, but her voice was not heard, so that
Eli thought that she was drunk and said to her, "How long will you act
like a drunken woman? Put away your wine and go from the presence of
Jehovah." But Hannah answered, "No, my lord, I am an unhappy woman; I
have not drunk wine nor any strong drink, but I have been pouring out my
heart before Jehovah. Do not think that your servant is a wicked woman,
for I have gone on speaking until now because my grief and vexation are
so great." Eli answered, "Go in peace, and may the God of Israel grant
what you have asked of him." She said, "May your servant have your
approval!" So the woman went away and ate, and her face was no longer
sad.

Early in the morning she and her husband rose; and after they had
worshipped Jehovah, they returned to their home at Ramah. In the course
of the year Hannah had a son and named him Samuel, saying, "I asked him
of Jehovah."

Elkanah and all his household again went to offer the yearly sacrifice
to Jehovah, but Hannah did not go up, for she said to her husband, "When
the child is weaned, then I will take him, and he shall go to Jehovah's
temple and live there the rest of his life." Elkanah said to her, "Do
what seems best to you; wait until you have weaned him; only may Jehovah

help you to do what you have promised."

So the woman waited and nursed her son until she weaned him. Then she took him with her, and a three-year-old ox, a bushel of flour, and a skin of wine, and brought him to the temple of Jehovah at Shiloh. Then they killed the ox, and Hannah brought the child to Eli and said, "Oh, my lord, as surely as you live, I am the woman who stood near you here praying earnestly to Jehovah. This is the boy for whom I prayed. Jehovah has granted what I asked of him. Therefore I have given him to Jehovah; as long as he lives he belongs to Jehovah."

Elkanah returned to his home in Ramah, but the boy stayed to serve Jehovah under the direction of Eli the priest. So Samuel--a young boy dressed in a linen robe--did the duties of a priest in the temple. His mother also made him a little robe and each year brought it to him when she came up with her husband to offer the yearly sacrifice.

Eli blessed Elkanah and said, "Jehovah repay you with children from this woman for the gift which she has given to Jehovah." Then they returned to their home; and Hannah had three more sons and two daughters. Meantime the boy Samuel grew up in the temple of Jehovah.

The sons of Eli were very wicked. They knew not Jehovah, and they despised the offerings which were brought to him. Eli was very old, and whenever he heard that his sons were doing wrong he said to them, "Why do you do such things, for I hear of your wicked deeds from all the people. No, my sons: it is not a good report that I hear from the people of Jehovah." But they did not listen to the words of their father.

The boy Samuel grew and won the favor both of Jehovah and of men. He continued to serve Jehovah under the direction of Eli; but in those days not many messages came from Jehovah.

One day Eli was lying in his room. His eyes had begun to grow dim so that he could not see. While the lamp of God was still burning, and Samuel was lying in the temple of Jehovah where the ark of God was, Jehovah called, "Samuel! Samuel!" He answered, "Here am I." Then he ran to Eli and said, "Here am I, for you called me." But Eli said, "I did not call, lie down again." So he went and lay down. Then Jehovah called again, "Samuel! Samuel!" Samuel rose and went to Eli and said, "Here am I, for you called me." But Eli answered, "I did not call, my son; lie down again."

Now Samuel did not yet know Jehovah nor had a message from Jehovah been given to him. So when Jehovah called Samuel again the third time, he rose and went to Eli and said, "Here am I, for you called me!" Then Eli knew that Jehovah was calling the boy. So he said to Samuel, "Go, lie down, and if you are called, say, 'Speak, Jehovah, for thy servant is listening.'" So Samuel went and lay down in his place.

Then Jehovah came and called as at other times, "Samuel! Samuel!" And Samuel answered, "Speak, for thy servant is listening." Jehovah said to Samuel, "See, I am about to do a thing in Israel that will make the ears of every one who hears it tingle. On that day I will do to Eli all that

I have said that I would do to his family from the first to the last. For I have told him that I will punish his family forever for the crime of which he knew his sons were guilty, for they did not do what God commanded and he did not stop them."

Samuel lay until morning, and then he opened the doors of the temple of Jehovah. He was afraid to tell the vision to Eli. But when Eli called him and said, "Samuel, my son," he said, "Here am I." Eli asked, "What is the thing that Jehovah said to you? Keep nothing from me; may God do to you whatever he will, if you keep from me a word of all that he said to you." So Samuel told him everything, and kept nothing from him. And Eli said, "It is Jehovah; let him do what seems good to him."

THE ARK AMONG THE PHILISTINES

In those days the Israelites went out to meet the Philistines, and in a hard-fought battle the Israelites were defeated by the Philistines.

When the people returned to the camp, the leaders of Israel said, "Why has Jehovah let us be beaten to-day by the Philistines? Let us bring the ark of our God from Shiloh. He may then go out with us and deliver us from our enemies."

So the people sent to Shiloh and took from there the ark of Jehovah of hosts. When it came to the camp, all the Israelites shouted so loud that the earth resounded.

The Philistines heard the sound of the shouting and said, "What does this sound of great shouting in the camp of the Hebrews mean?" When they knew that the ark of Jehovah had come to the camp, they were afraid, for they said, "Their god has come to their camp. Woe to us! for it has never been so before; but be strong and act like men." So the Philistines fought, and the Israelites were defeated and each fled to his tent.

The same day a Benjamite from the ranks ran to Shiloh with his clothes torn and with earth on his head. As he came, Eli was sitting on his seat by the gate watching the road, for his heart was trembling for the ark of God.

When the man came and told the people of the city, they all cried out. Eli heard the sound of crying and said, "What is this uproar?" So the man came quickly and told Eli, "I am the man who came from the battle, for I fled from the ranks." Eli said, "How did it go, my son?" The messenger answered, "Israel fled from the Philistines, and many people were killed, and your two sons are dead, and the ark of God has been captured." When he spoke of the ark of God, Eli fell off his seat backward beside the gate, and his neck was broken, for he was old and heavy, and he died.

The Philistines took the ark of God and brought it to the temple of Dagon in Ashdod and set it up by the side of Dagon. When the people of Ashdod rose early the next day and came to the temple of Dagon, there was Dagon on the ground flat on his face before the ark of Jehovah. Then they raised up Dagon and set him in his place again. But when they rose early on the following morning, there was Dagon on the ground flat on his face before the ark of Jehovah. The head of Dagon and both his hands were broken off on the door sill, and only his body was left.

Jehovah severely punished the people of Ashdod, for he punished them with boils. When the men of Ashdod saw this, they said, "The ark of the god of Israel shall not stay with us, for he is severely punishing us and Dagon our god." So they sent for all the rulers of the Philistines and asked, "What shall we do with the ark of the god of Israel?" They answered, "Let it be carried around to Gath."

So they carried the ark of the God of Israel around to Gath. Then Jehovah punished the men of that city, both young and old, with boils. Therefore they sent the ark of the God of Israel to Ekron; but when it came to Ekron, the Ekronites cried out, "They have brought around the ark of the god of Israel to kill us and our people!" They sent, therefore, and gathered all the rulers of the Philistines and said, "Send the ark of the god of Israel back to its own place, so that it will not kill us and our people!"

Then the Philistines called the priests and diviners and asked, "What shall we do with the ark of Jehovah? Tell us with what we shall send it to its place." They said, "If you send back the ark of the god of Israel, you must not send it away empty, but must return to him an offering to repay him for all that you have done to the ark. Then you shall be healed, and you shall know why he has continued to punish you." They said, "What offering shall we send back in order to repay him?"

They said, "Five golden boils and five golden mice, the same number as the rulers of the Philistines; for one plague was upon you as well as upon your rulers. Now therefore prepare a new cart and two milch cows that have never worn a yoke, and fasten the cows to the cart, but leave their calves behind them at home. Then take the ark of Jehovah and place it upon the cart and put in a box at its side the golden objects which you are sending to them as an offering to repay him. Then send it away. If it goes on the way to its own border, to Bethshemesh, then it is Jehovah who has done us this great harm; but if not, then we shall know that it is not he who has punished us; it was only an accident."

The men did so, and the cows took a straight course along the Bethshemesh road. They went along the highway, lowing as they went, and did not turn aside to the right nor to the left. The rulers of the Philistines also went after them as far as Bethshemesh.

The inhabitants of Bethshemesh were harvesting their wheat in the valley, and when they looked up and saw the ark, they rejoiced at the sight. When the ark came into the field of Joshua, the Bethshemeshite, it stood still there. And a great stone was there; so they split up the wood of the cart and offered the cows as a burnt-offering to Jehovah. When the five rulers of the Philistines saw it, they returned to Ekron the same day.

HOW SAMUEL FOUND A LEADER

There was a rich Benjamite named Kish, who lived at Gibeah. He had a son named Saul, a man full grown and handsome; no one among the Israelites was more handsome than he. From his shoulders and upward he was taller than any of the people.

Now the asses of Kish, Saul's father, were lost. So Kish said to Saul, "Take one of the servants with you and go, look for the asses." They went through the highlands of Ephraim and the land of Shalishah, but did not find them. Then they crossed into the land of Shaalim, but the asses were not there. They also went through the land of Benjamin, but did not find them.

They had come into the land of Zuph when Saul said to his servant who was with him, "Come, let us go back, that my father may not stop thinking of the asses and be anxious about us." The servant answered him, "There is a man of God in this town who is held in honor; all that he says is sure to come true. Now let us go there; perhaps he can tell us the way we should go."

Saul said to his servant, "But, suppose we go, what shall we take to the man, for the bread is gone from our sacks, and there is no present to take to the man of God? What have we?" The servant answered Saul again and said, "See, I have with me a quarter of a silver shekel. Give it to the man of God that he may tell us our way." Then Saul said to his servant, "Your advice is good; come, let us go." So they went to the town where the man of God was.

As they were going up to the town, they met young women going out to draw water and said to them, "Is the seer here?" They answered them, "He is there; he is before you. Make haste, for he has just come into the town, for the people have a sacrificial feast to-day at the sacred place on the hilltop. As soon as you come to the town, you will find him before he goes up to the high place to eat, for the people will not eat until he comes, for he blesses the sacrifice, and then the guests eat. Therefore go up now, for at this time you will find him."

So they went up to the town, and when they came inside the gate, Samuel was just coming out toward them to go up to the high place. Now Jehovah had told Samuel the day before Saul came, "About this time to-morrow I will send you a man out of the land of Benjamin, and you shall anoint him to be a prince over my people Israel. He shall deliver my people from the power of the Philistines; for I have seen the suffering of my people, because their cry has come to me."

When Samuel saw Saul, Jehovah told him, "This is the man of whom I spoke to you! He it is who shall rule over my people." So when Saul met Samuel in the gate, and said, "Tell me, if you will, where the seer's house is," Samuel answered Saul, "I am the seer; go up before me to the high place, for you shall eat with me to-day; and in the morning I will let you go and will tell you all that is in your mind. As for your asses that were lost three days ago, do not trouble yourself about them for they have been found. And to whom belongs all that is best in Israel? Does it not belong to you and to your father's house?" Saul answered and said, "Am I not a Benjamite, of the smallest of the tribes of Israel, and is not my family the least of all the families of the tribe of Benjamin? Why then do you speak to me in this way?"

But Samuel took Saul and his servant and brought them into the hall and made them sit at the head of the guests (who were about thirty in number). Samuel also said to the cook, "Bring the part which I gave you and told you to put aside." So the cook took up the leg and what was on it and placed them before Saul. Then Samuel said, "See what has been kept for you! Set it before you and eat, for it was kept for you until the appointed time, that you might eat with the people whom I have invited." So Saul ate with Samuel that day.

After they came down from the high place into the town, they spread a bed for Saul on the roof, and he lay down. Then at daybreak Samuel called to Saul on the roof, saying, "Rise, that I may send you away." So Saul rose, and he and Samuel went out into the street. As they were going out of the town, Samuel said to Saul, "Tell the servant to go on before us, but you stand here that I may tell you the message from God."

Then Samuel took the flask of oil and poured it on Saul's head, and kissed him and said, "Has not Jehovah anointed you to be a prince over his people Israel? You shall rule over Jehovah's people and deliver them from the power of their enemies on every side. This is the sign that Jehovah has anointed you to be a prince over his own people: when you go from me to-day you shall find two men at Rachel's tomb; and they will say to you, 'The asses that you went to seek are found, and now your father is thinking no more about the asses but is worrying about you, saying, "What shall I do for my son?"' Then you shall go on from there and come to the oak of Tabor. There three men going up to God at Bethel will meet you, one carrying three kids, another carrying three loaves of bread, and another carrying a skin of wine. They will greet you and give you two loaves of bread which you shall take from their hand. After that you shall come to Gibeah. As you come to the city you will meet a band of prophets coming down from the high place with a lyre, a tambourine, a flute, and a harp before them, while they prophesy. Then the spirit of Jehovah will come suddenly upon you, and you shall prophesy with them, and shall be changed into another man. When these signs come to you, do whatever you can, for God is with you." So when Saul turned away from Samuel, God gave him a new heart, and all those signs came to pass that day.

Saul's uncle also said to him and to his servant, "Where did you go?" He said, "To seek the asses; and when we saw that they were not to be found, we went to Samuel." Saul's uncle said, "Tell me what Samuel said to you." Saul replied, "He told us that the asses were surely found." But Saul did not tell him that Samuel had said he should become the ruler.

After about a month, Nahash, the Ammonite, came up and besieged Jabesh in Gilead; and all the men of Jabesh said to Nahash, "Make terms with us and we will serve you." But Nahash, the Ammonite, said to them. "On this condition will I make terms with you: that I bore out the right eye of each of you, and so bring disgrace upon all Israel." The elders of Jabesh said to him, "Let us have seven days in which to send messengers through all the land of Israel. Then, if there are none to save us, we will come to you."

So the messengers came to Gibeah where Saul lived and told the facts in the hearing of the people, and they all set up a loud wail. Just then Saul was coming from the field behind the oxen, and he said, "What is the trouble with the people that they are wailing?" Then they told him what the men of Jabesh had said. When he heard it, the spirit of Jehovah came suddenly upon him and he became very indignant. He took a pair of oxen, cut them in pieces, and sent them through all the land of Israel by messengers, who said, "Whoever does not come out after Saul and after Samuel, the same shall be done to his oxen!"

Then a terror from Jehovah fell upon the people, and they all gathered together. And Saul said to the messengers who came, "Say to the men of Jabesh in Gilead, 'To-morrow by the time the sun grows hot help shall come to you.'"

So the messengers went and told the men of Jabesh, and they were glad. Therefore the men of Jabesh said to the Ammonites, "To-morrow we will come out to you, and you shall do to us whatever you please." So on the following day, Saul divided the people into three divisions; and they went into the midst of the camp early in the morning, and fought against the Ammonites until noon. The Ammonites who stayed behind were so scattered that not two of them were left together.

Then all the people went to Gilgal and there in the presence of Jehovah made Saul their ruler, and they offered sacrifices there to Jehovah; and Saul and all the men of Israel were very happy.

JONATHAN'S BRAVE DEED

Saul picked out three thousand men from the Israelites. Two thousand were with Saul in Michmash and on the highland of Bethel, and a thousand were with his son Jonathan in Gibeah. But Saul had sent the rest of the people each to his home.

Then Jonathan attacked the company of the Philistines in Gibeah; and the Philistines heard of it. But Saul sounded a call to arms throughout all the land, saying, "Let the Hebrews hear!" So all Israel heard the report that Saul had attacked the Philistines, and also that Israel was hated by them.

Then the Philistines were gathered together to fight with Israel: three thousand chariots, six thousand horsemen, and foot soldiers as many as the sand of the seashore. They came up and camped in Michmash. When the men of Israel saw that they were in a tight place (for the people were hard pressed), the people hid themselves in caves, in holes, in the rocks, in tombs, and in pits. Also many people crossed over the Jordan to the land of Gad and Gilead.

Then Saul counted the people who were with him and found that there were about six hundred men. And Saul and his son Jonathan, together with the people who were with them, remained in Gibeah, while the Philistines camped in Michmash. Then the Philistines came out of the camp in three divisions to steal whatever they could find: one division turned toward

Ophrah, in the land of Shual, another toward Bethhoron, and another toward the hill that looks down over the valley of Zeboim. But the garrison of the Philistines went out to the pass of Michmash.

Now on that day Jonathan the son of Saul said to the young man who carried his armor, "Come, let us go over against the Philistines' garrison that is on the other side." But he did not tell his father.

Meantime Saul was sitting just outside of Gibeah under the pomegranate-tree which is near the threshing-floor, and there were with him about six hundred men. But the people did not know that Jonathan had gone.

Along the ravine by which Jonathan tried to go over against the Philistines there was a steep rock on one side, and a steep rock on the other; one was named The Shining, and the other The Thorny. One rock rose up north of Michmash, and the other south of Geba.

So Jonathan said to the young man who carried his armor, "Come, let us go over to the camp of these heathen Philistines. Perhaps Jehovah will act for us, for there is nothing that can keep Jehovah from delivering his people either by many or by few." His armor-bearer replied, "Do whatever you wish, I will do my best to help you." Then Jonathan said, "See, we will cross over to the men and show ourselves to them. If they say to us, 'Stand still until we can reach you,' then we will stand still in our place, and will not go up to them. But if they say, 'Come up to us,' then we will go up; for this shall be the proof that Jehovah has given them into our power."

When both of them showed themselves to the Philistines, the Philistines said, "There are Hebrews coming out of the holes where they have hidden." So they called to Jonathan and his armor-bearer, "Come up to us, and we will show you something!" Then Jonathan said to his armor-bearer, "Come up after me, for Jehovah has given them into the power of Israel."

So Jonathan climbed up on his hands and feet and his armor-bearer after him. And the Philistines fell before Jonathan, and his armor-bearer followed and put them to death. In the first attack Jonathan and his armor-bearer killed about twenty men with spears and rocks from the field. Then there was a great panic in the camp, in the open field, and among all the Philistines. Even those who were out robbing were panic-stricken, and the earth quaked, so that it produced a God-sent panic.

The watchmen of Saul in Gibeah looked and saw the great company of Philistines melting away and rushing here and there. Then Saul said to the people who were with him, "Look now and see who is gone from us." When they searched they found that Jonathan and his armor-bearer were not there. So Saul said to Ahijah, "Bring the ark of God here," for at that time it was with the Israelites. While Saul was still speaking to the priest, the noise and disorder among the Philistines kept on increasing. Therefore, Saul said to the priest, "Do not wait to consult Jehovah!"

Then Saul and all the people that were with him gathered together and went into battle. And every Philistine's sword was turned upon his fellow, so that there was a very great confusion among them. The Hebrews who once were on the side of the Philistines and who had joined their army also went over to the side of the Israelites who were with Saul and Jonathan. Likewise all the men of Israel who were hiding in the highlands of Ephraim, when they heard that the Philistines had fled, closely followed them in the battle. So Jehovah delivered Israel that day, and the battle passed over beyond Bethhoron. But Saul made a great mistake that day, for he strictly commanded the people, saying, "The man who shall eat any food until evening and until I take vengeance on my enemies shall be punished." So none of the people tasted food.

Now there was honey on the surface of the ground; and when the people came to the forest, they saw a stream of honey, but no one put his hand to his mouth, for the people feared the punishment. But Jonathan had not heard when his father commanded the people. Therefore he reached out the end of the staff that was in his hand and dipped it in the honeycomb and put his hand to his mouth, and he felt refreshed. Then one of the people spoke up and said, "Your father strictly commanded the people, saying, 'The man who eats food this day shall be punished.'" But Jonathan replied, "My father has brought great trouble on the land. See how I have been refreshed because I tasted a little of this honey. If only the people had eaten freely to-day of the spoil of their enemies, many more of the Philistines would have been slain."

Then Saul said, "Let us go down after the Philistines by night and take spoil until daybreak, and let us not leave one of them." They said, "Do whatever you think best." But the priest said, "Let us ask of God." So Saul asked of God, "Shall I go down after the Philistines? Wilt thou deliver them over to Israel?" But he did not answer him that day. Therefore Saul said, "Come here, all you leaders of the people, and find out who has done wrong to-day. For as surely as Jehovah the deliverer of Israel lives, even though it be Jonathan my son, he shall die." But not one of the people answered him.

Then he said to all Israel, "You be on one side, and I and Jonathan my son will be on the other." The people said to Saul, "Do what you think best." Therefore Saul said, "Jehovah, God of Israel, why hast thou not answered thy servant this day? If the sin be mine or that of Jonathan my son, Jehovah, God of Israel, show it by the lot marked Urim; but if the sin lies with thy people Israel, show it by the lot marked Thummim." Then the lot fell on Jonathan and Saul and not on the people. So Saul said, "Cast the lot between me and Jonathan my son. He whom Jehovah selects must die." The people said to Saul, "It shall not be so!" But Saul made the people do as he said, and they cast the lot between him and Jonathan his son; and it fell on Jonathan.

Then Saul said to Jonathan, "Tell me what you have done." So Jonathan told him, "I did indeed taste a little honey with the end of the staff that was in my hand. Here I am! I am ready to die." Saul said, "God do so to me and more too; Jonathan, you shall surely die!" But all the people said to Saul, "Shall Jonathan die who has brought this great deliverance to Israel? Far from it! As surely as Jehovah lives, not one hair of his head shall fall to the ground, for he has done this day what God wished." So the people saved Jonathan from death.

DAVID'S VICTORY OVER THE GIANT

As long as Saul lived there was bitter war with the Philistines. Whenever Saul saw a strong or able man, he would take him into his service.

Now the spirit of Jehovah had left Saul and an evil spirit from Jehovah troubled him. So Saul's servants said to him, "See now, an evil spirit from Jehovah is troubling you. Let your servants who are here advise you, and let them seek a man skilled in playing the lyre. Then, whenever the evil spirit comes upon you, he shall play on the lyre, and you will be well." Saul said to his servants, "Find me a man who plays well, and bring him to me."

Then one of the young men said, "I have seen a son of Jesse the Bethlehemite who is a skilled musician, a strong and able man, a soldier, careful in speech, handsome, and Jehovah is with him." So Saul sent messengers to Jesse with the command, "Send me David your son, who is with the flock."

Then Jesse took ten loaves of bread, a skin of wine, and a kid, and sent them to Saul by his son David. So David came to Saul and entered his service; and Saul loved him and he became his armor-bearer. Saul sent this message to Jesse: "Let David remain in my service, for I am well pleased with him." And whenever the evil spirit from God came upon Saul, David would take the lyre and play, and Saul would breathe more easily and would be well, and the evil spirit would depart from him.

Now the Philistines gathered their forces for war, and camped between Socoh and Ezekah in Ephesdammim. Saul and the men of Israel came together and camped in the valley of Elah; and they were drawn up ready for battle against the Philistines.

The Philistines were standing on the hill on one side, and the Israelites were standing on the hill on the other side with the valley between them. Then there came out from the ranks of the Philistines a champion named Goliath, who was about ten feet tall. He had a helmet of bronze on his head and wore a bronze breastplate of scales which weighed one hundred and fifty pounds. He also had bronze greaves upon his legs and a bronze back-plate between his shoulders. The shaft of his spear was like a weaver's beam, and the head of his iron spear weighed about twenty pounds; and his shield-bearer went before him.

He stood and called to the ranks of Israel: "Why have you come out to form the line of battle? Am I not a Philistine and you servants of Saul? Choose a man for yourselves and let him come down to me. If he is able to fight with me and kill me, then we will become your servants; but if I conquer and kill him, then you shall become our servants and serve us." The Philistine added, "I defy the ranks of Israel to-day; give me a man that we may fight together."

When Saul and all the Israelites heard these words of the Philistine, they were terrified. But David said to Saul, "Let not my lord's courage fail him; I will go and fight this Philistine." Saul said to David, "You are not able to go and fight against this Philistine, for you are only a youth and he has been a warrior from his youth." But David said to Saul, "Your servant kept his father's sheep, and whenever a lion or a bear came and took a lamb out of the flock, I would go out after him and kill him and rescue it from his mouth. If he attacked me, I would seize him by his throat and kill him with a blow. Your servant has killed both lion and bear. Now this heathen Philistine shall be like one of them, for he has defied the armies of the living God. Jehovah who saved me from the paw of the lion and from the paw of the bear will save me from the hand of this Philistine." So Saul said to David, "Go, and may Jehovah be with you."

Saul clothed David with his own garments, and put a helmet of bronze on his head and gave him a coat of mail. And David fastened on his sword over his coat and was not able to walk, for he was not used to them. So he said to Saul, "I cannot go with these, for I am not used to them." So David took them off.

Then he took his club in his hand, and he chose five smooth stones from the bed of the brook and put them in his bag, and he took his sling in his hand and drew near to the Philistine. When the Philistine looked and saw David, he despised him, for he was but a fair and ruddy youth. So the Philistine said to David, "Am I a dog that you come against me with a club?" And he cursed David by his gods, and said, "Come to me that I may give your flesh to the birds of the heavens and to the beasts of the field."

Then David answered the Philistine, "You come to me with a sword and spear and javelin, but I come to you in the name of Jehovah of hosts and of the God of the armies of Israel whom you have insulted this day. Jehovah will deliver you into my hand that I may kill you and cut off your head."

When the Philistine started to attack him, David put his hand into his bag and took from it a stone, and slung it and struck the Philistine in the forehead. The stone sank into his forehead, and he fell on his face to the earth. Then David ran and stood over the Philistine, and drawing his sword from its sheath, he killed him and cut off his head with it.

When the Philistines saw that their champion was dead, they fled. The men of Israel and of Judah rose up and raised the battle-cry and followed the Philistines to the entrance to Gath and to the gates of Ekron, so that the wounded of the Philistines fell all the way from the battle-field even to Gath and Ekron.

SAUL'S MEAN JEALOUSY

When the Israelites and David returned from slaying the Philistines, the women came out from all the cities of Israel, singing and dancing, to meet Saul with tambourines, with cries of rejoicing, and with cymbals. The women sang gaily to each other and said,

> "Saul has slain his thousands,
> And David his tens of thousands."

Saul was very angry, for their words displeased him, and he said, "To David they give credit for ten thousands, but to me only thousands; what more can he have but the rulership?" So Saul kept his eye on David from that day onward. Saul feared David and did not let him stay near him. He made him commander over a thousand men; and David went out and came in at the head of the soldiers. In all that he did David acted wisely and had success, for Jehovah was with him. When Saul saw that he acted wisely, he was still more afraid of him. But all Israel and Judah loved David, for he went out and came in at their head.

Michal, Saul's daughter, also loved David, and when they told Saul, he was pleased, for he said, "I will give her to him, that she may lead him to destruction and that the Philistines may capture him." So Saul commanded his servants, "Say to David secretly: 'See, the ruler is pleased with you and all his servants love you; now therefore become his son-in-law.'" When Saul's servants told this to David, he said, "Do you think it easy for me to become the son-in-law of a ruler when I am poor and have no reputation!" When Saul's servants told him David's answer, he commanded, "Say to David: 'Saul wishes no price for his daughter except the proof that you have killed a hundred Philistines;'" for Saul thought that David would be killed by them.

So David went with his men and killed a hundred Philistines; and Saul gave him his daughter Michal as his wife. Then Saul knew that Jehovah was with David and that all Israel loved him, so he feared David still more.

Then Saul commanded his son Jonathan and all his servants to put David to death. But Jonathan was very fond of David. And Jonathan spoke well of David to Saul his father and said to him, "Do not sin against your servant David, for he has not wronged you and his behavior toward you has been excellent; for he risked his life and killed the Philistine, so that Jehovah saved all Israel. You saw it and rejoiced. Why then will you sin by shedding innocent blood in killing David without cause?"

So Saul listened to Jonathan and gave his solemn promise: "As surely as Jehovah lives, he shall not be put to death."

Then Jonathan called David and told him all these things. And Jonathan brought David to Saul and he was with him as before.

But there was war again, and David went out and fought against the Philistines and killed so many of them that they fled before him. Then an evil spirit from Jehovah came upon Saul while he was sitting in his house with his spear in his hand and while David was playing on the lyre. Saul tried to pin David to the wall with the spear, but David slipped away so that Saul drove the spear into the wall; and David fled and so escaped.

That night Saul sent messengers to David's house to watch him, so as to kill him in the morning. But Michal, David's wife, told him, "If you do not save your life to-night, you will be killed to-morrow." So Michal let David down through the window; and he fled away and escaped. Then Michal took the household god and laid it in the bed, and she put a pillow of goat's hair under its head and covered it with a garment. And when Saul sent messengers to seize David, she said, "He is sick."

Again Saul sent the messengers to the house of David with the command, "Bring him up to me on the bed, that I may put him to death." When the messengers came in, there was the household god in the bed with the pillow of goat's hair under its head. Saul said to Michal, "Why have you deceived me thus and let my enemy go?" Michal answered Saul, "He said to me: 'Let me go; why should I kill you?'"

JONATHAN'S LOVE FOR DAVID

Then David went and found Jonathan and said, "What have I done? What is my guilt, and what is my sin in the mind of your father, that he is seeking my life?" Jonathan replied, "No, no! You shall not die. You know that my father does nothing great or small that he does not tell me, and why should my father hide this from me? He surely will not." David answered, "Your father well knows that you are fond of me, and he is saying to himself, 'Do not let Jonathan know this that he may not be grieved.' But as surely as Jehovah lives and as you live, there is only a step between me and death."

Then Jonathan said to David, "What do you wish me to do for you?" David answered, "To-morrow is the festival of the New Moon and I ought to sit at the table with Saul, but let me go and I will hide myself in the field until evening. If your father misses me, then say, 'David asked permission of me to run to Bethlehem, his native town, for the yearly sacrifice is there for all his family.' If he says, 'Good,' then it is well with your servant; but if he gets angry, then you will know that he is planning to harm me. Now show kindness to your servant, for in the presence of Jehovah you have made a solemn agreement with your servant. But if I am at all guilty, kill me yourself, for why should you bring me to your father?" Jonathan said, "That shall never be! If I learn that my father is planning to do you harm, I will tell you."

Then David said to Jonathan, "Who will tell me if your father answers you harshly?" Jonathan answered, "Jehovah the God of Israel be witness that about this time to-morrow I will find out how my father feels. If he feels kindly toward you, then I will send and tell you. Should my father wish to do you harm, God do to Jonathan whatever he will and more too if I do not tell you and send you away that you may go in peace. May Jehovah be with you, as he has been with my father. And if I am yet alive, O may you show me kindness like that of Jehovah himself! But if I should die, you must never cease to be kind to my family. And if, when Jehovah destroys all the enemies of David from the face of the earth, the family of Jonathan should be destroyed by the family of David, may Jehovah punish the crime by the hand of David's enemies." So Jonathan renewed his solemn promise to David, because he loved him; for he loved him as much as he loved his own life.

Then Jonathan said to him, "To-morrow is the festival of the New Moon and you will be missed, for your seat will be empty. On the third day, when you will be greatly missed, go to the place where you hid yourself when my father attacked you, and sit down beside the heap of stones. I will shoot three arrows on one side of it, as though I shot at a mark. Then I will send the boy, saying, 'Go, find the arrows.' If I call to the boy, 'See, the arrows are on this side of you; pick them up!'--then come; for all goes well with you, and as surely as Jehovah lives, there is nothing to fear. But if I call to the boy, 'See, the arrows are beyond you,' then go, for Jehovah sends you away. And as for the promises which you and I have made, Jehovah is witness between you and me forever."

So David hid himself in the field; and when the festival of the New Moon came, Saul sat down at the table to eat. He sat on his seat, as usual,

by the wall, and Jonathan sat opposite, and Abner sat beside Saul; but

David's seat was empty. Saul, however, did not say anything that day,

for he thought, "It is an accident."

But on the next day when David's place was again empty, Saul said to

Jonathan, "Why has not the son of Jesse come to the table, either

yesterday or to-day?" Jonathan answered, "David asked permission to go

to Bethlehem, for he said, 'Let me go, for we have a family sacrifice in

the town, and my brother has commanded me to be there. Now if you

approve, let me go away that I may see my family.' Therefore, he has not

come to your table."

Then Saul's anger was aroused against Jonathan, and he said to him, "Son

of a rebellious slave girl! Do I not know that you are making the son of

Jesse your friend to your own shame and to your mother's shame? For as

long as the son of Jesse lives, neither you nor your rule will be safe.

Therefore, send now and bring him to me, for he is doomed to die."

Then Jonathan answered Saul his father and said, "Why should he be put

to death? What has he done?" But Saul flung his spear at him to strike

him. So Jonathan knew that his father had made up his mind to put David

to death. And Jonathan rose from the table in hot anger and ate no food

on the second day of the month, for he felt hurt because his father had

insulted David.

The next morning Jonathan went out into the field to the place agreed upon with David, and a small boy was with him. He said to his boy, "Run, find now the arrows which I shoot." As the boy ran, he shot an arrow beyond him. When the boy came to the place where the arrow which Jonathan had shot lay, Jonathan called to him, "Is not the arrow beyond you? Hurry, be quick, do not stop!" So Jonathan's lad gathered up the arrows, and brought them to his master. But the boy knew nothing about the signal. Only Jonathan and David understood.

THE COST OF A LIE

Then David went to Nob, to Ahimelech the priest who came trembling to meet David and said to him, "Why are you alone, and no one with you?" David answered Ahimelech the priest, "Saul has given me orders about some business and has said to me, 'Let no one know anything about the business on which I am sending you and about which I have given you orders.' I have also directed the young men to meet me at a certain place. Therefore, if you have at hand five loaves of bread, give them to me or whatever can be found." The priest answered David, "There is no plain bread at hand, but only holy bread." So the priest gave him holy bread, for there was no other bread there except that which had been removed from the temple to be replaced at once by hot bread.

Now Doeg, the Edomite, the chief of Saul's herdsmen, was there that day. And David said to Ahimelech, "Have you not here at hand a spear or sword? For I did not bring my sword or my weapons with me, since the king's business required haste." The priest said, "The sword of Goliath the Philistine whom you slew in the valley of Elah is there, wrapped in a cloth. If you wish to take that, do so, for there is no other except that here." David answered, "There is none like that; give it to me."

Then David went from there and escaped to the stronghold of Adullam. When his brothers and all his father's clan heard of it, they went down there to him. Every one who was in trouble and every one who was in debt, and every one who was discontented gathered about him, and he became their leader. About four hundred men were with him.

When Saul heard that David and the men with him had been found, he was
sitting in Gibeah, under the tamarisk-tree at the high place, with his
spear in his hand. And all his servants were standing about him. Saul
said to his servants who stood about him, "Hear, O Benjamites! Will the
son of Jesse give all of you fields and vineyards? Will he make all of
you commanders of thousands and commanders of hundreds? Is it not true
that all of you have plotted against me so that no one tells me that my
son has made an agreement with the son of Jesse, and that none of you
has pity upon me or tells me that my son has made my servant David my
enemy as he now is?" Then Doeg the Edomite, who was standing by the
servants of Saul, spoke up and said, "I saw the son of Jesse go to Nob,
to Ahimelech, the son of Ahitub. And the priest inquired of God for him
and gave him food and the sword of Goliath the Philistine."

Then Saul sent for Ahimelech the priest, and all his family and the
priests who were in Nob; and all of them came to him. Then Saul said,
"Listen, son of Ahitub!" He answered, "Here I am, my lord!" Saul said to
him, "Is it not true that you and the son of Jesse have plotted against
me and that you have given him bread and a sword and have inquired of
God for him, that he might rebel against me?" Ahimelech answered Saul,
"Who among all your servants is trusted like David, your son-in-law,
chief over your subjects, and honored in your household? Is this the
first time I have inquired of God for him? Far be it from me to be
disloyal! Do not think that I or any of my clan have any evil intention,
for your servant does not know the slightest thing about all this." But

Saul said, "Ahimelech, you shall surely die, you and all your family."

Then Saul said to the guards who were standing about him, "Turn and kill the priests of Jehovah, for they have plotted with David; and although they knew that he was fleeing, they did not tell me." But Saul's servants would not raise their hands to kill the priests of Jehovah. Then Saul said to Doeg, "Turn and kill the priests." So Doeg, the Edomite, turned and killed them. On that day he killed eighty-five men who wore the priestly robes.

But Abiathar, one of the sons of Ahimelech, escaped and fled to David. When Abiathar told David that Saul had killed the priests of Jehovah, David said to him, "I knew that day, because Doeg the Edomite was there, that he would surely tell Saul. I myself am responsible for the death of all your family. Stay with me, have no fear, for whoever seeks your life must first take mine, for you are placed in my charge."

A SOLDIER WHO SPARED HIS ENEMY

Now when David was told, "The Philistines are fighting against Keilah and are robbing the threshing-floors," he inquired of Jehovah, "Shall I go and attack these Philistines?" Jehovah said to David, "Go, attack the Philistines and save Keilah." But David's men said to him, "See, we are afraid here in Judah; how much more will we be if we go to Keilah against the armies of the Philistines?" When David again inquired of Jehovah, Jehovah answered him, "Arise, go down to Keilah, for I will give the Philistines into your hand." So David and his men went to Keilah and fought with the Philistines and drove away their cattle and killed a great many of them. In this way David delivered the people of Keilah.

Now when Abiathar, the son of Ahimelech, fled to David in Keilah, he came down with the priestly robe used in consulting Jehovah in his hand. And when Saul was told that David had come to Keilah, Saul said, "God has given him into my power, for by entering a town that has doors and bars he has let himself be trapped."

So Saul called all the people to arms to go down to Keilah to besiege David and his men. But when David knew that Saul was plotting evil against him, he said to Abiathar the priest, "Bring here the priestly robe." Then David said, "O Jehovah, the God of Israel, thy servant has surely heard that Saul is planning to come to Keilah, to destroy the town because of me. Will Saul come down, as thy servant has heard? O

Jehovah, God of Israel, tell thy servant." Jehovah said, "He will come down." Then David said, "Will the men of Keilah turn me and my men over to Saul?" Jehovah said, "They will." Then David and his men, who were about six hundred, left Keilah, and wandered from one place to another. When it was reported to Saul that David had escaped from Keilah, he no longer followed him. So David lived in the Wilderness of Ziph and stayed in the mountain strongholds.

Then the Ziphites came to Saul at Gibeah, saying, "Is not David hiding in the hill country of Hachilah?" So Saul went down to the Wilderness of Ziph with three thousand men of Israel to hunt for David. And Saul camped in the hill country of Hachilah; but David stayed in the wilderness. When David saw that Saul was following him into the wilderness, he sent out scouts and learned that Saul had come to the place just in front of him. David then arose and went to the place where Saul had camped. And he saw the place where Saul lay, with Abner the son of Ner, the commander of his army; and Saul was within the barricade, and the people were camped about him.

Then David turned to Ahimelech the Hittite and to Abishai the son of Zeruiah, Joab's brother, and said, "Who will go down with me to Saul's camp?" Abishai said, "I will go with you." So David and Abishai came to the people by night, and Saul was lying asleep inside the barricade, with his spear stuck into the earth at his head and with Abner and the soldiers lying about him.

Then Abishai said to David, "God has given your enemy to you to-day. Now let me pin him to the earth with his spear at one stroke, for I will not need to strike him twice!" David replied, "As surely as Jehovah lives, either Jehovah will smite him, or his day will come to die, or he will go down into battle and meet his end. Jehovah forbid that I should harm him whom Jehovah has called to rule! But now take the spear that is at his head and the jug of water, and let us go." So David took the spear and the jug of water from Saul's head, and they departed. But no man saw it or knew it, for they were all asleep, and no one awoke, for a deep sleep from Jehovah had fallen upon them.

Then David went across and stood on the top of a hill at a distance with a great space between them. And David called to the soldiers and to Abner, the son of Ner, and said, "Do you make no answer, Abner?" Abner answered, "Who are you that calls?" David said to Abner, "Are you not a man, and who is like you in Israel? Why then have you not kept guard over your lord the ruler of Israel? For one of the people came to destroy your lord. You have not done what is right. As surely as Jehovah lives you ought to be put to death, for you have not kept watch over your master whom Jehovah has called to rule. Now see where his spear is and his jug of water that was at his head."

Saul knew David's voice and said, "Is this your voice, my son David?" David replied, "It is my voice, my lord." And he added, "Why is it that my lord is following his servant? For what have I done? Or of what am I guilty? Now therefore let my lord listen to me. If Jehovah has stirred you up against me, let him accept an offering. But if men have stirred you up against me, let them be cursed before Jehovah, for they have driven me out to-day, saying, 'Go serve other gods,' so that I have no share in the land which Jehovah has given to his people. May I not meet my end far away from the presence of Jehovah, for the ruler of Israel has come out to seek my life, as one hunts a partridge on the mountains."

Then Saul said, "I have done wrong. Come back, my son David, for I will do you no more harm, for you have spared my life to-day. I have acted foolishly and have made a great mistake." David answered, "Here is Saul's spear! Let one of the young men come over and take it. May Jehovah reward each one who does right and is faithful; for Jehovah gave you to me to-day, but I would not harm one whom Jehovah had called to rule. Just as your life was of great value in my sight so may my life be of great value in Jehovah's sight, and may he deliver me from all trouble."

Then Saul said to David, "May you be blessed, my son David! You shall do great deeds and shall surely succeed!" So David went his way, but Saul returned home.

ABIGAIL'S SENSIBLE ADVICE

Then David went away into the Wilderness of Maon. Now there was a man in Maon, whose property was in Carmel. The man was very rich; he had three thousand sheep and a thousand goats, and he was shearing his sheep at Carmel. His name was Nabal, and his wife's name was Abigail. The woman was sensible and beautiful, but the man was rough and ill-mannered; and he was a Calebite.

When David heard in the wilderness that Nabal was shearing his sheep, he sent ten young men with the command, "Go up to Carmel and enter Nabal's house and greet him in my name. You shall say to him and to his family, 'Peace and prosperity be to you and your family and to all that you have. Now I have heard that you have sheep-shearers. Your shepherds were with us, and we did not insult them, and nothing of theirs was missing all the while they were in Carmel. Ask your young men and they will tell you. Therefore receive my young men favorably, for we have come on a feast-day. Give also whatever you have at hand to your servants and to your son David.'"

When David's young men came, they spoke to Nabal for David as they were told, and then waited. But Nabal answered David's servants, "Who is David? And who is the son of Jesse? Many are the slaves these days who break away from their masters! Should I then take my bread and my water and my meat that I have prepared for my shearers and give it to men of whom I know nothing?" So when David's young men returned and told him, he said to them, "Let every man put on his sword." So they all put on their swords. David also put on his sword; and about four hundred men followed David, and two hundred stayed with the baggage.

But one of the young men told Abigail, Nabal's wife, "David has just sent messengers from the wilderness to greet our master, but he insulted them. The men have been very good to us and we have not been harmed nor have we missed anything, as long as we were with them in the open country. They were as a wall about us both night and day all the time we were near them guarding the sheep. Now therefore decide what you will do, for evil is planned against our master and against all his household, for he is such an ill-tempered man that no one can say a word to him."

Then Abigail quickly took two hundred loaves of bread, two skins of wine, five roasted sheep, five baskets of parched grain, a hundred bunches of raisins, and two hundred cakes of figs, and loaded them on asses. She said to her young men, "Go on ahead of me; see, I am coming after you." But she said nothing about it to her husband Nabal. As she was riding on the ass and coming down under cover of a hill, David and his men were coming down toward her, so that she met them. David had just said, "It was in vain that I guarded all that belongs to this fellow in the wilderness, so that nothing of his was missing, for he has returned me evil for good. May God bring a similar judgment upon David and more too, if by daybreak I leave a single man of all those who belong to him."

When Abigail saw David, she dismounted quickly from her ass and bowed down before him with her face to the ground. As she fell at his feet she said, "Upon me, my lord, upon me be the blame. Only let your servant speak to you, and listen to her words. Let not my lord pay any attention to that mean man Nabal, for as his name is, so is he. 'Fool' is his name and folly rules him. But your servant did not see the young men of my lord, whom you sent. Now, my lord, as surely as Jehovah lives and as you live, since Jehovah has kept you from murder and from avenging yourself by your own hand, may your enemies and those who seek to harm my lord be like Nabal. Let this present which your servant has brought to my lord be given to the young men who follow him. I beg of you, forgive the wrong done by your servant, for Jehovah will certainly make my lord's family strong, for my lord is fighting for Jehovah, and you shall not be guilty of any evil deed as long as you live. Should a man rise up to pursue you and seek your life, Jehovah your God will care for you, but he will cast away the lives of your enemies as from a sling. When Jehovah has done for you all the good that he has promised and has made you ruler over Israel, you will not have to be sorry that you shed blood without cause or that you were revenged by your own hand. When Jehovah gives prosperity to my lord, then too remember your servant."

David said to Abigail, "Blessed be Jehovah the God of Israel, who sent you this day to meet me, and blessed be your good sense. A blessing on you, who have kept me this day from murder and from avenging myself by my own hand. For as surely as Jehovah the God of Israel lives, who has kept me from doing you harm, unless you had quickly come to meet me, truly by daybreak not one man would have been left to Nabal."

So David received from her all which she had brought him. And he said to her, "Go back in peace to your house. See, I have listened to your advice and granted your request."

When Abigail returned to Nabal, he was holding a feast in his house like a king. He was feeling merry, for he was very drunk; so she told him nothing whatever until daybreak. But in the morning, when the effects of the wine were gone, his wife told him what she had done. Then his heart stopped beating and he became like a stone. About ten days later he had a stroke from which he died.

When David heard that Nabal was dead, he said, "Thanks be to Jehovah who has punished Nabal's insult to me and has kept me from doing wrong, for Jehovah has visited Nabal's crime upon his own head."

Then David sent to ask Abigail to become his wife. When his servants came to her at Carmel and said, "David has sent us to you to take you to him to be his wife," she rose and bowed her face to the earth and said, "See, your slave is willing to be even a servant to wash the feet of my lord's servants." Then Abigail quickly rose and mounted an ass; and five of her maids followed as servants. So she went with the messengers of David, and became his wife.

MAKING THE BEST OF TROUBLE

Then David said to himself, "I shall be killed some day by the hand of
Saul. There is nothing better for me than to escape into the land of the
Philistines. Then Saul will give up hope and search no more for me in
all the land of Israel; and so I will escape from him." David,
therefore, with the six hundred men who were with him went over to
Achish, king of Gath. And David and his men lived with Achish at Gath,
each with his family. When Saul was told that David had fled to Gath, he
gave up looking for him.

David said to Achish, "If now you will grant me the favor, give me a
place in one of the towns in the open country, that I may live there;
for why should your servant live in the royal city with you?" So Achish
gave him Ziklag, and David lived in the open country of the Philistines
a year and four months.

And David and his men went up and made a raid upon the Geshurites, the
Girzites, and the Amalekites; for these tribes live in the land which
extends from Telem to the land of Egypt. As often as David made a raid
on the land, he did not leave alive man or woman, but taking the sheep,
the oxen, the asses, the camels, and the clothing, he returned and went
to Achish. Then when Achish said, "Where have you made a raid to-day?"
David answered, "Against the South Country of Judah, or against the
South Country of the Jerahmeelites, or against the South Country of the
Kenites." And Achish trusted David, thinking, "He has made his people

Israel hate him; therefore he will be my servant forever."

Now in those days the Philistines gathered their forces to make war against Israel. And Achish said to David, "You and your men shall surely go with me in the army." David replied, "You shall then know what your servant can do." Achish said to David, "In that case I will make you the captain of my body-guard from this time on."

Then the Philistines gathered all their forces at Aphek, and the Israelites camped at the fountain in Jezreel. When the rulers of the Philistines were marching past, by hundreds and by thousands, and David and his men were marching in the rear with Achish, the commanders of the Philistines said, "What are those Hebrews doing here?" Achish said to them, "Is this not David, the servant of Saul the ruler of Israel, who has been with me these two years, and I have found no fault in him from the time that he came to me to the present?"

But the commanders of the Philistines were displeased and said to him, "Send the man back to the place where you had stationed him. Do not let him go down with us into battle, lest we have a foe in the camp; for how could this fellow better win back the favor of his master than with the heads of these men? Is not this the David of whom they sang to one another in the dances:

"'Saul has slain his thousands,
And David his ten thousands?'"

Then Achish called David and said to him, "As surely as Jehovah lives, you are upright, and your conduct toward me both in and out of the camp has been satisfactory, for I have found nothing wrong in you from the time that you came to me to the present; but you are not trusted by the other rulers. Go back home, therefore, in peace, that you may do nothing to displease the rulers of the Philistines." David said to Achish, "But what have I done? What have you found in your servant from the day that I entered your service, that I may not go out and fight the enemies of my lord the king?" Achish answered, "I know that you are as faithful to me as an angel of God, but the commanders of the Philistines have said, 'He shall not go with us into battle.' Therefore, you and those who came with you are to rise early in the morning, and go to the place where I have stationed you. Do not plan any evil, for I trust you, but rise early in the morning and, as soon as it is light, depart."

So David and his men arose early in the morning to return to the Philistine land, but the Philistines went up to Jezreel.

On the third day, when David and his men returned to Ziklag, the Amalekites had made a raid on the South Country and on Ziklag, and had attacked Ziklag and burned it with fire, and had also carried away captive all who were in it, including the women and children. They had not killed any but had carried them away with them. Then David and the people who were with him wept aloud until they were no longer able to weep.

David was in great trouble, for the people spoke of stoning him, because they all felt bitter, having lost their sons and daughters: but David took courage, for he trusted in Jehovah his God. So David with his six hundred followers went on to the Brook Besor, where those who were too tired to cross the brook stayed behind.

They found there an Egyptian in the open field and brought him to David and gave him food to eat and water to drink. Then David said to him, "To whom do you belong, and where do you come from?" He replied, "I am an Egyptian lad, an Amalekite's servant, and my master left me behind because three days ago I fell sick. We marched into the South Country of the Cherethites and into that which belongs to Judah and into the South Country of Caleb, and Ziklag we destroyed by fire." David said to him, "Will you guide me to this robber band?" He replied, "Swear to me by your God, that you will neither kill me nor turn me over to my master, and I will guide you to this band."

When he had brought him down, the Amalekites were scattered over all the land, eating and drinking and dancing, because of all the great spoil that they had taken from the land of the Philistines and from the land of Judah. David fought against them from twilight to the evening of the next day, and only four hundred young men who were mounted on camels escaped.

So David took from the Amalekites all that they had carried away and rescued his two wives; nothing at all was missing. Then he took all the flocks and the herds and drove those animals before the people, and they said, "This is David's spoil."

When David came to the two hundred men who had been so faint that they could not follow him, all the wicked, mean fellows who went with him said, "Because these men did not go with us, let us not give them any of the spoil that we have taken, except that each man may take his wife and children and depart." David answered, "My brothers, you shall not do so with that which Jehovah has given us, after he has saved our lives and given this robber band that attacked us into our power. Those who stay with the baggage shall have an equal share with those who fight." So from that day to the present he made this a law and a rule in Israel.

When David came to Ziklag, he sent some of the spoil to the leaders of Judah and to his relatives, saying, "See! a present for you from the spoil of the enemies of Jehovah."

THE DEATH OF TWO BRAVE WARRIORS

Samuel had died and all Israel had mourned for him and had buried him in his own town Ramah. Saul, too, had put the mediums and those who had messages from the spirits of the dead out of the land.

Then the Philistines came and camped in Shunem, and Saul gathered all the Israelites and camped in Gilboa. But when he saw the army of the Philistines, he was terrified and filled with fear. So he asked of Jehovah whether he should go against them, but Jehovah did not answer him either by dream or by lot or by the prophets. Then Saul said to his servants, "Find for me a woman who is a medium, that I may go and ask through her." His servants said to him, "There is such a woman at Endor."

So Saul did not let any one know who he was, but put on other clothes and went, taking two men with him. And they came to the woman at night. He said, "Ask for me through some departed spirit and bring up for me the one for whom I shall ask." The woman said to him, "You know what Saul has done, how he has driven from the land the mediums and those who have messages from the spirits of the dead. Why then are you trying to catch me, to put me to death?" But Saul swore to her by Jehovah, saying, "As surely as Jehovah lives, no punishment will come to you from this act." Then the woman said, "Whom shall I bring up to you?" Saul said, "Bring up Samuel."

When the woman saw Samuel, she screamed and said to Saul, "Why have you deceived me, for you are Saul?" Saul replied, "Do not be afraid! What do you see?" The woman said to Saul, "I see a god coming out of the earth." Saul asked, "What does he look like?" She said, "An old man is coming up, and he is wrapped in a cloak." Then Saul knew that it was Samuel; and he bowed with his face to the earth and worshipped.

Samuel said to Saul, "Why have you disturbed me by bringing me up?" Saul answered, "I am in great trouble, for the Philistines are making war against me, and God has turned from me and answers me no more, neither by prophets nor by dreams. So I have called you to tell me what I shall do." Samuel said, "Why do you ask of me when Jehovah has turned from you and become your enemy? He has taken the authority from your hand and given it to another, even to David. To-morrow you, with your sons beside you, shall fall, and Jehovah will deliver the army of Israel into the power of the Philistines."

Then Saul fell at full length upon the earth, for the words of Samuel filled him with fear, so he had no strength left, for he had not eaten any food all that day and night. When the woman came to Saul and saw that he was in great trouble, she said to him, "See, I have taken my life in my hand and have done what you asked me. Now therefore, listen also to my advice and let me set before you a little food, and eat that you may have strength to go on your way." Saul refused and said, "I will not eat"; but his servants, as well as the woman, urged him, until he listened to their advice. Then he rose from the earth and sat upon the couch. And the woman had a fat calf in the house which she quickly killed. And she took flour and kneaded it and baked from it bread without yeast. She set it before Saul and his servants, and they ate. Then they rose up and went away that night.

The Philistines fought against Israel, but the Israelites fled from them and fell dead on Mount Gilboa. Then the Philistines closely followed Saul and his sons; and they killed Jonathan and Abinadab and Malchishua, the sons of Saul. So the battle went against Saul, and when the archers found out where he was, he was severely wounded. Then Saul said to his armor-bearer, "Draw your sword and kill me with it, so that these heathen Philistines may not come and make sport of me." But his armor-bearer would not, for he was very much afraid. Saul, therefore, took his own sword and fell upon it. When his armor-bearer saw that Saul was dead, he also fell upon his sword and died with him. So Saul and his three sons and his armor-bearer died on the same day.

When the Israelites who were in the towns of the lowland and across the Jordan saw that the Israelites had fled and that Saul and his sons were dead, they left their towns and fled, and the Philistines came and took them.

On the next day, the Philistines came to rob the dead, and found that Saul and his three sons had fallen on Mount Gilboa. They cut off his head and stripped off his armor and sent messengers through all the land of the Philistines to bring the good news to their idols and to the people. And they put his armor in the temple of Ashtarte and fastened his body on the wall of Bethshan.

When the inhabitants of Jabesh in Gilead heard what the Philistines had done to Saul, their brave men rose up and marched all night, and they took the bodies of Saul and his sons from the wall of Bethshan and brought them to Jabesh and mourned over them there. Then they took their bones and buried them under the oak-tree in Jabesh and ate no food for seven days.

On the third day after David returned to Ziklag, after defeating the Amalekites, a man came from the camp of Saul with his clothes torn and with earth upon his head. When he came to David, he fell on the ground before him. David said to him, "Where do you come from?" He answered, "I have escaped from the camp of Israel." David said to him, "How did the battle go? Tell me." He answered, "The people fled from the battle-field, and many of them fell, and Saul and Jonathan his son are dead!"

Then David and all the men who were with him tore their clothes and mourned and wept and went without food until evening, because Saul and Jonathan his son and the people of Jehovah had fallen by the sword.

David then sang this dirge over Saul and Jonathan:

"Weep, O Judah!
Grieve, O Israel!
On your heights are the slain!
How the mighty have fallen!

"Saul and Jonathan, beloved and lovely!
In life and in death they were never parted;
They were swifter than eagles,
They were stronger than lions.

"O Jonathan, your death has mortally wounded me,
O Jonathan, my brother, for you I am sorrowing.
You were ever a friend to me most dear,
Your love meant far more than the love of women!

"How the mighty have fallen,
And the weapons of war vanished!"

A SHEPHERD BOY WHO WAS CALLED TO LEAD A NATION

After this David asked of Jehovah, "Shall I go up into one of the towns of Judah?" Jehovah answered, "Go up." When David asked, "To which shall I go?" he said, "To Hebron." So David went up with his two wives, Ahinoam and Abigail. And David brought the men who were with him, each with his family, and they lived in the towns about Hebron. Then the men of Judah came there and made David ruler over the people of Judah.

When they told David about the men of Jabesh in Gilead who had buried Saul, David sent messengers to them and said, "May you be blessed by Jehovah because you have shown this kindness to your master Saul and have buried him. Even so may Jehovah show kindness and faithfulness to you. I also will repay you for this kind deed which you have done. Therefore be brave and courageous; for Saul your master is dead, and the people of Judah have made me ruler over them."

Now Abner, the commander of Saul's army, had taken Ishbaal the son of Saul and brought him over to Mahanaim and made him ruler over Gilead and all Israel. But the people of Judah remained loyal to David.

There was constant war between the followers of Saul and those of David. But David kept growing stronger while the followers of Saul grew weaker.

Then Rechab and Baanah, the sons of Rimmon, went about midday to the palace of Ishbaal, as he was taking his rest at noon. The doorkeeper of the palace was cleaning wheat, but he grew drowsy and slept. So Rechab and Baanah his brother slipped in and, attacking Ishbaal, they killed him and cut off his head.

Then all the tribes of Israel came to David at Hebron and said, "See, we are your relatives. When Saul was ruler over us, it was you who led the Israelites, and Jehovah has said to you, 'You shall be shepherd of my people Israel, and you shall become the leader of Israel.'" So all the leading men of Israel came to David, and he made an agreement with them in Hebron in the presence of Jehovah, and they made David ruler over Israel. David was thirty years old when he began to rule and he ruled forty years.

When the Philistines heard that they had made David ruler over Israel, all the Philistines went up to search for David; but when he heard of this he went down to the fortress.

Three of David's thirty warriors went down to him to the top of the rock, to the fortress of Adullam, while a force of the Philistines was camped in the Valley of Rephaim. David was at that time in the fortress, and a company of the Philistines was in Bethlehem. And David said, longingly, "O that some one would bring me a drink of water from the well of Bethlehem which is near the gate!" Then the three famous warriors broke through the line of the Philistines and drew water out of the well of Bethlehem which was near the gate and brought it to David. He would not drink of it, however, but poured it out as an offering to Jehovah and said, "Jehovah forbid that I should drink it. This is the blood of the men who went at the risk of their lives." Therefore he would not drink it.

When the Philistines came and spread out over the Valley of Rephaim, David asked of Jehovah: "Shall I go out against the Philistines? Wilt thou give them into my hand?" Jehovah said to David, "Go; for I will certainly give the Philistines into your hand." So David went to Baal-perazim, and defeated them there; and he said, "Jehovah has broken down my enemies before me, like waters which break through their banks."

Then the Philistines came up again and spread out over the Valley of Rephaim. When David asked of Jehovah, he said, "You shall not make a direct attack. Go around behind them and attack them opposite the balsam-trees. When you hear the sound of marching in the tops of the balsams, act quickly, for then Jehovah will have gone out before you to overthrow the army of the Philistines." David did as Jehovah commanded him and drove the Philistines from Gibeon as far as Gezer.

JERUSALEM MADE THE CAPITAL CITY

David and his men went to Jerusalem against the Jebusites, the people of the land who had said to David, "You shall not come in here, for the blind and the lame will turn you back," for they thought, "David cannot come in here."

But David took the fortress of Zion, and lived there. He also built a wall around it, and called it the City of David.

David continued to grow more powerful, for Jehovah of hosts was with him. And Hiram, king of Tyre, sent messengers to him, and cedar-trees and carpenters and masons, and they built a palace for him. So David knew that Jehovah had made him ruler over Israel and his kingdom powerful for the sake of his people Israel.

David again gathered all the chief men of Israel, thirty thousand in all, and went with all the people to Baal-Judah, to bring up from there the ark of God. They placed the ark of God upon a new cart and brought it out of the house of Abinadab on the hill. Uzzah and Ahio, the sons of Abinadab, guided the cart. Uzzah went beside the ark of God, while Ahio went before it. David and all the people of Israel danced before Jehovah with all their might to the music of harps and lyres and drums and castanets and cymbals.

When they came to the threshing-floor of Nachon, Uzzah stretched out his hand to hold up the ark of God, for the oxen stumbled. Then the anger of Jehovah was aroused against Uzzah and he struck him down there, because he had stretched out his hand to the ark; so he died there in the presence of God. David was afraid of Jehovah that day, and said, "How can the ark of Jehovah come to me?" So David was not willing to remove the ark of Jehovah to the City of David, but carried it aside to the house of Obed-edom, the Gittite, and it remained there three months. But Jehovah blessed Obed-edom and all his family.

When the report came to David, "Jehovah has blessed Obed-edom and all his family because of the ark of God," David joyfully brought up the ark from the house of Obed-edom to the City of David. When the bearers of the ark of Jehovah had gone six paces, David offered an ox and a fat animal as a sacrifice; and he danced before Jehovah with all his might, and he had about his waist a priestly garment made of linen. So David and all the house of Israel brought up the ark of Jehovah with shouting and the blare of trumpets.

When they had brought in the ark of Jehovah and had set it in its place in the tent that David had built for it, he offered burnt-offerings and sacrifices to Jehovah. When David had finished offering these sacrifices, he blessed the people in the name of Jehovah of hosts and gave to each of the many Israelites who were there, to both men and women, a roll of bread, a portion of meat, and a cake of raisins. Then all the people went back to their homes.

This message also from Jehovah came to Nathan, the prophet: "You shall say to my servant David: 'Jehovah of hosts declares, I took you from the pasture from following the sheep to be chief over my people Israel. I have been with you wherever you went, to destroy all your enemies before you, and I will make you a name, like that of the great in the earth. When your life is ended and you are buried with your fathers, I will raise up your son after you, and I will make his rule strong. I will be a father to him, and he shall be my son. When he goes astray I will gently correct him. I will not withdraw my favor from him as I withdrew it from Saul. Your house and your dominion shall always stand firm before me; your authority shall stand forever.'"

DAVID'S KINDNESS TO JONATHAN'S SON

Then David asked, "Is any one left of the family of Saul to whom I may show kindness for Jonathan's sake?" And there was a servant of Saul named Ziba. When they called him before David, he said to him, "Are you Ziba?" He replied, "Your servant." David said, "Is there any one else belonging to the family of Saul to whom I may show kindness like that which God shows to us?" Ziba answered, "A son of Jonathan is still living, but he is lame in his feet." David inquired, "Where is he?" Ziba replied, "He is in the house of Machir in Lodebar."

Then David sent and brought him from the house of Machir; and when Meribaal the son of Jonathan came to David, he bowed down to the ground before him. David said, "Meribaal!" He answered, "Here is your servant!" David said to him, "Fear not, for I will surely show you kindness for the sake of your father Jonathan, and I will give back to you all the land of your grandfather Saul; and you shall always eat at my table." Meribaal bowed down and said, "What is your servant that you should look favorably upon one as unworthy as I?"

Then David called to Ziba, Saul's servant, and said to him, "I have given to your master's son all that belongs to Saul and to his family. You with your sons and servants shall cultivate the land for him and harvest the fruits, that your master's son may have food to eat; but Meribaal, your master's son, shall always eat at my table." Now Ziba had fifteen sons and twenty servants; and he said to David, "Your servant will do all that my lord commands."

So Meribaal ate at David's table like one of his own sons. Meribaal also
had a young son, whose name was Mica. And all who lived in the house of
Ziba were Meribaal's servants. So Meribaal lived in Jerusalem, and
though he was lame in both feet, he always ate at David's table.

A RICH MAN WHO WAS A THIEF

One evening, while Joab was besieging Rabbath Ammon, David rose from his bed and walked upon the roof of the royal palace. From the roof he saw a woman bathing; and she was very beautiful. And David sent to ask about the woman; and some one said, "Is not this Bathsheba, the wife of Uriah the Hittite?" Then David sent messengers to bring her; and she came to him, but later returned to her home.

Then David wrote a letter to Joab and sent it by Uriah. In the letter, he said, "Place Uriah in the front line where there is the fiercest fighting, then draw back from behind him, that he may be struck down and die." So Joab, in posting guards over the city, sent Uriah to the place where he knew there were brave men. When the men of the city went out to fight against Joab, some of the soldiers of David fell, and Uriah the Hittite was killed.

Then Joab sent to tell David all about the war, and he gave this command to the messenger: "If, after you have finished telling the ruler all about the war, he is angry and says to you, 'Why did you go so near to the city to fight? Did you not know that they would shoot from the wall? Who struck down Abimelech the son of Jerubbaal? Did not a woman cast an upper millstone upon him from the wall, so that he died at Thebez? Why did you go near the wall?' then say, 'Your servant Uriah the Hittite is dead also.'"

So the messenger of Joab went to Jerusalem and told David all that Joab commanded him. Then David said to the messenger, "Say to Joab, 'Let not this thing trouble you, for the sword takes one and then another. Go on fighting against the city and capture it,' and encourage him."

When Bathsheba heard that Uriah her husband was dead, she mourned for him as was the custom. When the mourning was over, David sent for her, and she became his wife and she had a son.

What David had done displeased Jehovah and he sent the prophet Nathan to David. Nathan went to him and said, "There were two men in one city, the one rich and the other poor. The rich man had many flocks and herds; but the poor man had nothing except one little ewe lamb which he had bought. He fed it, and it grew up with him and with his children. It used to eat of his own small supply of food and drink out of his own cup, and it lay in his bosom and was like a daughter to him.

"Now a traveller came to the rich man; and he spared his own flock and did not take an animal from it nor from his own herd to make ready for the traveller who had come to him, but took the poor man's lamb and prepared it for the guest who had come."

Then David was very angry, and he said to Nathan, "As surely as Jehovah lives, the man who has done this deserves to die; he shall repay seven times the value of the lamb, because he showed no pity."

Nathan said to David, "You are the man! Jehovah the God of Israel declares: 'I made you ruler over Israel and I delivered you out of the hand of Saul. I gave you your master's house and your master's wives to be your own, and I gave you the nations of Israel and Judah. If that were too little, I would add as much again. Why have you despised Jehovah by doing that which is wrong in his sight? You have struck down Uriah the Hittite with the sword, and have taken his wife to be your wife, and have killed him with the sword of the Ammonites. Now, therefore, the sword shall never cease to smite your family, because you have despised me and have taken the wife of Uriah the Hittite to be your wife.'"

David said to Nathan, "I have sinned against Jehovah!" Then Nathan said to David, "Jehovah has also put away your sin so that you shall not die. Yet, because by this deed you have shown contempt for Jehovah, the child that is born shall surely die." Then Nathan went to his house.

And Jehovah smote Bathsheba's child so that it fell sick. David prayed to God for the child, and ate no food but went in and lay all night in sackcloth upon the earth. The older men in his house stood over him to raise him up from the earth; but he would not rise nor eat with them. When on the seventh day the child died, the servants of David were afraid to tell him that the child was dead, for they said, "While the child was yet alive, we spoke to him and he paid no attention to our voice. How can we tell him that the child is dead, for he will do some harm!"

But when David saw that his servants were whispering together, he knew that the child was dead, and said to his servants, "Is the child dead?" They replied, "He is dead." Then David rose from the earth, washed and put oil on himself, changed his clothes, and went into the temple of Jehovah and worshipped. After that he went to his own house; and he asked for bread, and when they set it before him, he ate.

His servants said to him, "What is this you have done? You ate no food and cried for the child while it was alive, but when the child died, you rose and ate bread." He replied, "While the child was yet alive, I ate no food and cried aloud, for I said, 'Who knows whether Jehovah will have mercy, so that the child will live?' But now that he is dead, why should I eat no food? Can I bring him back? I am going to him, but he will not come back to me."

ABSALOM THE UNGRATEFUL SON

Some time later Absalom, David's son, prepared a chariot and horses and fifty men to run before him. He used to rise early and stand beside the highway which led to the city gate. He would call to him every man who had a suit that was to come before the ruler for judgment and say, "Of what city are you?" When the man replied, "Your servant is from one of the tribes of Israel," Absalom would say to him, "Your claims are good and right; but the ruler has not appointed any one to hear you. Oh, that some one would make me judge in the land, so that every man who has any complaint or cause would come to me, and I would see that he received justice!" And whenever a man came near to bow before him, he would put out his hand and take hold of him and kiss him. In this way Absalom treated all the Israelites who came to David for justice. Thus, Absalom stole from David the hearts of the Israelites.

At the end of four years, Absalom said to his father, "I should like to go and keep my promise, which I have made to Jehovah in Hebron." David said to him, "Go in peace." So he went to Hebron; but Absalom sent messengers to all the tribes of Israel to say, "As soon as you hear the sound of the trumpet, cry, 'Absalom has become ruler in Hebron.'" With Absalom there went two hundred men from Jerusalem, who were invited and went innocently, knowing nothing at all of what he was going to do. Absalom also sent for Ahithophel, David's adviser, from the city of Giloh, while he was offering the sacrifices. And the plot was strong, for more and more people kept going over to Absalom.

When a messenger came to David, saying, "The hearts of the men of Israel
have gone over to Absalom," David said to all his servants who were with
him at Jerusalem, "Up, let us flee; for, if we do not, none of us will
escape from Absalom. Go at once, or he may quickly overtake us and bring
evil upon us and kill the people of the city." Then David's servants
said to him, "It shall be done as our lord wishes; we are your
servants."

So David and all the people who followed him went out and stood at the
last house, while all the officers and the royal body-guard and all the
men of Ittai the Gittite, the six hundred who had followed him from
Gath, passed on before him.

Then David said to Ittai, "Why do you also go with us? Go back and stay
with the new ruler, for you are a foreigner and away from your own land.
Yesterday you came, and to-day shall I make you go up and down the land
with us, while I go where I may? Go back and take your men with you, and
may Jehovah show you kindness and faithfulness." But Ittai answered, "As
surely as Jehovah lives and as my lord the ruler of Israel lives,
wherever my lord is, whether dead or living, there your servant will
be!" David said to Ittai, "March on." So Ittai marched on with all his
men and with all the children who were with him.

All the people were weeping aloud while David stood in the Kidron
valley, and they went by before him on the way to the wilderness. And
Zadok and Abiathar came carrying the ark of Jehovah and set it down

until all the people had passed. Then David said to Zadok, "Carry the ark of God back into the city. If I win Jehovah's favor, he will bring me back and show me both it and the place where he dwells. But if he declares, 'I have no trust in you, then here am I, let him do to me as he thinks best.'" So Zadok and Abiathar carried the ark of God back to Jerusalem and stayed there.

But David went up, weeping as he climbed the Mount of Olives with his head covered and his feet bare. All the people who were with him covered their heads and went up, weeping as they went.

And when David came to the summit, where one worships God, Hushai the Archite with his garment torn and earth upon his head, came to meet him. David said to him, "If you go on with me you will be a burden to me. But if you go back to the city, and say to Absalom, 'Your brothers have gone away and your father has gone after them; I will be your servant, O king; as I have been your father's servant in the past, so now I will be your servant,' you can defeat for me the advice of Ahithophel. And have you not there with you Zadok and Abiathar the priests? See, they have there with them their two sons, Ahimaaz, Zadok's son, and Jonathan, Abiathar's son. By them you shall send word to me of everything that you hear." So Hushai, David's friend, went into the city, when Absalom came to Jerusalem.

Then David and all the people who were with him, reached the Jordan tired out, but he refreshed himself there.

And Absalom, with all the men of Israel, came to Jerusalem, and Ahithophel was with him. When Hushai, David's friend, came to Absalom, Hushai said to him, "May the king live, may the king live!" But Absalom said to Hushai, "Is this your love for your friend? Why did you not go with your friend?" Hushai answered, "No! to him whom Jehovah and his people and all the men of Israel have chosen, to him will I belong and with him will I stay. Also whom should I serve? Should it not be his son? As I have served your father, so will I serve you."

The advice which Ahithophel gave in those days was thought by David and Absalom to be the same as if it had come from God himself. And Ahithophel said to Absalom, "Let me now pick out twelve thousand men, and set out and follow David to-night. Thus I will come upon him when he is tired and weak and will frighten him, and all the people who are with him will flee. Then I will kill only the king, and I will bring back all the people to you as the bride turns to her husband. Seek only the life of one man, and all the people will be at peace." This advice pleased Absalom and all the leaders of Israel.

Then Absalom said, "Call now Hushai and let us hear also what he has to say." When Hushai came to Absalom, Absalom said to him, "Thus Ahithophel has spoken; shall we act as he advises? If not, you advise us." Then Hushai said to Absalom, "The advice that Ahithophel has given this time is not good. You know that your father and his men are mighty warriors and are now angry, like a bear robbed of her cubs. Your father is also a soldier and will not stay at night with the people. Even now he has hidden himself in one of the caves or in some other place. If some of the people fall at first, whoever hears it will say, 'There is a slaughter among the people who follow Absalom.' Then even he who is brave, whose heart is like the heart of a lion, will completely lose courage; for all Israel knows that your father is a great warrior, and they who are with him are brave men. But I advise, let all the Israelites be gathered to you, from Dan to Beersheba, as many as the sand that is by the sea, with you yourself marching in the midst of them. In this way we will come upon him in some place where he will be found, and we will fall upon him as the dew falls on the ground; and of him and of all the men who are with him not even one shall be left. If he goes into a city, then all Israel will bring ropes to that city, and we will pull it down into the valley, until not even a small stone is found there."

Absalom and all the men of Israel said, "The advice of Hushai is better than the advice of Ahithophel." For Jehovah had planned to defeat the good advice of Ahithophel, so that Jehovah might bring evil upon Absalom.

Then Hushai said to Zadok and to Abiathar the priests, "This is what Ahithophel advised Absalom and the leaders of Israel; and this is what I advised. So now send quickly and say to David, 'Do not spend this night at the fords of the wilderness, but by all means cross over, for fear that David and all the people with him be killed.'"

Now Jonathan and Ahimaaz were staying at Enrogel; and a maid-servant was to go and bring them news, and they were to go and tell David, for they must not be seen coming into the city. But a boy saw them and told Absalom. Then they both went away quickly and entered into the house of a man in Bahurim, who had a well in his courtyard into which they descended. The women took and spread the covering over the mouth of the well, and scattered dried fruit upon it, so that nothing was known. And when Absalom's servants came to the woman at the house and said, "Where are Ahimaaz and Jonathan?" the woman answered, "They have gone over the brook." When they had searched and could find nothing, they returned to Jerusalem.

But as soon as the men had gone away, Ahimaaz and Jonathan came up out of the well, and went and told David and said, "Get up, cross quickly over the water, for so has Ahithophel advised in regard to you." Then David and all the people who were with him rose and crossed the Jordan. By daybreak there was not one left behind.

A BROKEN-HEARTED FATHER

After Absalom and all the men of Israel crossed the Jordan, David counted the troops who were with him, and put over them commanders of thousands and of hundreds. And he divided the troops into three divisions; one was under the command of Joab, another under Abishai, and another under the command of Ittai. Then David said to the people, "I too will surely go out with you." But the people said, "You shall not go out; for if we are defeated, or if half of us die, it will make no difference, for you are equal to ten thousand of us. It is therefore more important for you to be ready to help us from the city." David said to them, "I will do what you think best!" So he stood beside the gate, while all the troops marched out by hundreds and by thousands.

David commanded Joab and Abishai and Ittai, "Deal gently for my sake with the young man, with Absalom!" All the people heard when he gave the commanders this order about Absalom.

So the troops went out into the field against Israel. The battle was fought in the forest of Ephraim. And the soldiers of Israel were defeated there by those who were loyal to David, and the loss of life on that day was great--twenty thousand men. The battle spread over the whole country; and the dense thickets killed more people than were killed by the sword.

Absalom happened to meet the soldiers of David while riding upon his mule, and the mule went under the thick branches of a great oak, and

Absalom's head caught fast in the oak, and he was hung between heaven and earth, while the mule that was under him went on. A certain man saw it and told Joab, "I saw Absalom hanging in an oak." Joab said to the man who told him, "You saw him! Why did you not strike him to the ground? I would have given you ten pieces of silver and a belt." But the man said to Joab, "If I were to feel the weight of a thousand pieces of silver in my hand, I would not raise my hand against the ruler's son, for in our hearing he commanded you and Abishai and Ittai, 'Take care of the young man Absalom.' If I had treacherously taken his life, nothing would have been hidden from the ruler of Israel, and you yourself would not have tried to save me." Joab answered, "I will not waste time with you."

So he took three spears in his hand and drove them into Absalom's heart, while he was still alive in the midst of the oak. Then Joab said to a negro slave, "Go, tell the ruler of Israel what you have seen." And the negro bowed before Joab and ran off.

Now David was sitting between the two gates, and when the negro came, he said, "Let my lord receive the good news; Jehovah has punished for you this day all those who rose up against you.'" David said to the negro, "Is it well with the young Absalom?" The negro answered, "May the enemies of my lord and all who rebel against you to harm you be as that young man!"

Then David was very sad and went up to the chamber over the gate and wept. As he wept he said, "My son Absalom, my son, O my son Absalom! Oh that I had died for you, Absalom, my son, my son!" And it was reported to Joab, "The ruler of Israel is weeping and mourning for Absalom." So for all the people the victory that day was turned to mourning, because they heard that David was mourning for his son. Therefore, the people stole away into the city, as people who are ashamed steal away when they have run away in battle. But David covered his face and cried aloud, "My son Absalom, Absalom, my son, my son!"

www.ingramcontent.com/pod-product-compliance
Lightning Source LLC
Chambersburg PA
CBHW081156090426
42736CB00017B/3347